PENIS ENVY

Hannah Sloan

"When your plane is falling out of the sky, grab the dog leash."

Jeff

BYOB

I keep saying
there's no god
but
I'm suspecting he'll kill me soon
People will set their drinks down
on anything that's sticking out
You say goodnight
but I know you're going
somewhere else

PRE

Day four of the war
and my dick won't go down
No one cares
that you don't like the term
friendly fire

MEATEATER

You take the time to slick back your hair
and you have careful words
baiting
You baby talk me but I don't take offense
because your dogs get it too
You offer me nice rum in nice cups
Your dog's cone is scratching my legs and we're crying
We're blacked out before dinner
You crawl out my window in your button-down
Tell me
What did we eat

DEAD DOG

You begging
I thought I'd be into it
but you're sleeveless
because you think muscles have something
to do with it
It's raining and your hair is down
curls catching drops
they shake before they hit my dirty floor
I'm not into it but you insist
you need your t-shirts back
We are made to do each deed twice
Once for me and another for everyone else

YOU DRAG YOUR ARMS LIKE DONKEY KONG

In my dream all your teeth
are in the middle of your mouth
My new experiences make your dick bigger
but you love me less
You show me your roommate
doing his morning coffee enema
but it looks like you

ALL THE STARBURSTS ARE YELLOW
BUT SARAH'S PUSSY IS TITE TITE TITE

spring tits
baby limes
with pearly arrows pointing
up
asking god, asking me
do you know what happens when you die

PROGRESSIVE

I pet your cat while you
do dabs with your roommate
in another part of the house

TRIVIAL PURSUIT

when Tom Brady misses the ball
it becomes my fault
Do you wish I would get on top more?
When you take away the screens
there you are
a fucking empty pasta shell

2 AM

My bed isn't the same
without you, you moan
but your toilet paper lasts twice as long
You should melt some cheese on that meat
You should melt some cheese on that meat
It's dark
and we're both hungry

BUT WHAT IF

Tiny purses are in style now
and even worse, your dog is judging me
I decline ballroom dancing lessons
from a boy that goes by his middle name
and he spits saying *you're a drunk bitch*
on your untouchable cloud
but you're just a drunk bitch
bunny hopping around
a teddy bear with no face
Six months later big purses are in
slung around our bellies
I've got a lot of time Now
but not enough
to make him happy

THE SUMMER OF JEFF

Is your bed warm enough
with two green-haired girls
two lighters too?
Your pillow is as dirty as any
ten-year-old pillow and
her bottoms are drip-drying
in the shower

NOVEMBER

LA is burning and
I haven't updated my phone yet
the ATM is blinking
help
while the doctor's got his hand up
your ass
He can't remember the punchline
but it was very clever

PENIS ENVY

I shake you awake to ask
if you're hungry
want to smoke a bowl
will you take it in your mouth
you nod but when I blow
you spit and turn over
penis envy
brought on by my cramps
masturbating in the mirror
to get off
he says *If I had a small dick*
I'd show everyone!
I am his dog
he spits and my mouth waters
We wonder
do the monkeys miss their children
less
or are we just louder

HOT CHICKEN

HEY
IT'S TRISHA
IS EVERYTHING
KOSHER
RYAN PASSED OUT AND WE, WE
ARE BACK TOGETHER
I JUST SAW THOSE TEXTS
AND WAS WONDERING WHAT'S UP
HE'S UNCONSCIOUS OR ELSE
I WOULDN'T BE
BOTHERING
YOU

UPPERHAND

driving down the 101
begging you for your
silk long johns
It's not going to happen

THE FIRST TIME

Leaning on a marble counter
teetering
a quilted armchair
overstuffed
straddling pillow, paunch
every bloat in-between
groping
Can you look at yourself yet?
We listen to sad songs and
play with watercolors
but your stuffed bear is defiant
I don't want you

GOLDILOCKS

One bed
glass bending for these serious citizens
not to mention
plan b twice in one week
at least in your town they don't make them
impossible to open
with your teeth
Two beds pushed together
you're softer than I remember
You ask for *real* orange juice
We know it's not

27

You keep sending me nudes
You were so bad with words
I thought
it was poetry

I'm shitting in your shitty
bathroom
for the last time
and it feels
like every other time

YOUR BITCH MOM

My only job tonight
is getting this peach
home safe
pulpy
from where I grabbed too hard
seething
and soft
It has to be gone tomorrow

MOTHER'S MILK

Fuck I'm bleeding again
as you thrust into me
propped on palms and knees
white bedding smeared with brown
no body comes
you're shorter than I remember
dutifully you push
I grimace

You click your teeth
suck in a deep breath, violent thrust
release
You drive a yellow Hyundai that you call a sports car
wear Mickey Mouse boxers
You moan like a woman
like it's for me
You open the door
Whatever you want babe
and you tell me
Genghis Khan had a really nice vision of Europe
draping your arm around my waist
Once all the people are dead
tucking my hair behind my ear
It'll be a great place for all the horses

oh fuck oh my fucking
god baby
jesus shit
I look up mid-blow
your hand on your hips, head thrown
back
you look down at the ring of blood
around my mouth, crisping
at the corners
Better not to tell, you throw your head
back

2:18

Let me count the ways
Let me count your ribs
You're the boss I scream
but because I want to
I am not what you are
looking for
and as I choke him he croaks
You should love yourself more

SWEET TOOTH

The cookie tin my mom gave you
sits on top
of the sea green
cum rag on top of the clean laundry
We empty it
and think about other people

PIZZA MAN

I spend so much time
making other people's beds
in my own house
Who are you
and that fly that came
out of your newly gray hair
is moving so slowly
He saunters
down to the top corner of
my AC unit
Is it overconfidence
or is it love

THAT BABY WAS A WINE GLASS

I pull out my wallet
even though *he* asked *me*
No
I am not with this tiny leopard panty man and
Wouldn't you call me later?
A loud American in a coffee shop
complaining and smiling
Now we're in a pile of blankets behind a wardrobe
or a gun rack
agreeing with a stranger on the
sadness of a song
let's relish this tomorrow
He leaves the room and I say to you
dumbly
This is Love I think
you disagree
He was massaging you, sitting
on your spine
you were waiting for the knife
reliable and hard
thinking
that's why god gave us holes on every side
you whisper that a tailbone is poking you
We're both laughing but you let go first
Is he man or is he us
You are always smarter

SHAME

Your tiny Chinese pillow
sits on the floor
usually
I keep my retainer there
when I trust you

I'M NOT VERY FORMAL

After one curly fry, you light
a cig satisfied and say
OH
BUT WON'T YOU TRY THIS ROCK WITH ME
it'll shoot you to the moon ecstatic
waving your smoke signal
I should've asked you out years ago, you lament
but I've seen your friend's soft dick
and I'd rather not

OCTOBER

I start bleeding but we don't stop
My sheets are white but
they're not your sheets
In the morning Baby paints
You smoke
Can I have one
You smear brown blood in Baby's blueberry bowl
Baby grits her gums
and you want to know
What song is this

WWJD

They told us we'd live forever
but we were just looking
for some kids
to move our furniture for free
high scamming
waxing cornhole bolton
masturbating to shining butts on the tv

A GOOD GIRL

Jesus Christ
how did we get here
still as broke as last June
stop doing cocaine in my room
I know
it's the closest to the door
I can't tell you no
but you can't ever keep your beer upright
You can't ever keep track of your blow either
but we'll wait
for you to find it

BIG CITY

Shaking his hips
in front of his father
A vision of the city
hating waking
to see the sleep already gone
from someone else's eyes
he's been moving, doing
your brother
watching early morning cartoons
without you, and you're mad
You were so sure he was asleep

BORRACHA

U pull out ur tits
and make me think of James Joyce
cows lowing in the country
downtown
U buy us drinks and we wipe our mouths

UNTITLED

I saw you touch
that cardboard box
so tenderly
when you thought it was my leg

NOTHING GOOD

You ground me into
the black sand
from behind, grit on my lips
you spit and said
sorry for taking it too far
There's beds but we're in a bush
the morning chicken bus
I get on
and fall asleep standing up
You waving as the sun comes

GRAPES

The xmas tree goes up
and goes down
panting, we are still thinking
about the exes
me about a boy
I mean, *man*
who bought me that first edition
to hold over my head
You about the baby girl
with the baby
You say she's crazy but
that just makes me interested
We pull on our stone mothers
to maybe make them feel
but I don't see you leaving

STEPHANIE'S FINGER

belly button tighter
her eyes sharper
her yes
I haven't
loved him yet but I wonder
what he's doing
do we talk about forever
a taboo
her half moon crescents
happy
beaming up leftovers
you offer me an ice cream sandwich
for twelve bucks
my yes
nodding overdraft

555

You eat the best part of the cookie
and as I wipe the crumbs from bed
I hope I won't have to be here long
You think everything is a sign while
I am the yellow devil searching
creampie compilations and best loans for
bad credit
discreet the doorman
nods
He knows my favorite part
is watering my plants and
leaving you

BABY IN THE BORO

Lippy you say
Your honeypot is private
and dripping
cooling
You think you can love him
maybe
but
you push his head away
and pray to El Chapo
you don't die today

HOUSEFLY

There's a fly in the bathroom
someone I've seen before
A big one, he squints at me
from behind the curtain
I worry
he's building a house for my parents
while they worry
if I will ever get married
but never with that wart on my left hand
banking on black walnut orchards
The big payout
when you're dead
There's love
you calling me from the ATM line
but when it's your turn you hang up
Give me big coins
cherries
staining your hands

UNTITLED

You wash your hands in that house
and you'll smell like him forever

OUR DOWNSTAIRS NEIGHBOR

You're wearing your Michelangelo t-shirt
again
You're taking a picture of my ass
as I'm taking a picture of
your ass
We catch each other
in full butt underwear, evolving
eating watermelon
with two hands
sick, equipped with palm fronds
at the kids' table
stomping Mary Magdalene
Begging
Rhinestone Cowboy *let me in*
I can smell your dog, I know you're there
There's another tornado and cave crickets so
we go back to the cars to die
with diseases in our head
Our gynecologist asks us not to wear heels indoors
It makes it hard for her

YOU'RE ALL GETTING YOUR ASSES NUKED ANYWAY

I've never been called boo before
but I hope it's not today
Jerry bought a Tundra
to slang poon
Let me guess
Is it silver
She wants to go to SeaWorld bad
Most people miss the big show because
Ego
but Homeland Security dad will get you in
the water with Shamu
You're eating your cum
to cum closer
to god
Humor me
sulking in the sheets

MANOS

I've seen you
at sixty
and
I like
where your hands are

**I CAN TELL YOU DON'T LIVE HERE
BY THE WAY
YOU PICK UP THE NEWSPAPER**

I will hold it against you
your soft shoulders
the way you look
in my eyes when you're on top
forcing meaning
so I act like it hurts
bite your shoulder
a bean on its back

SUBARU

there is the feeling
of sitting in a station wagon with two people
saying *Mariah Carey is the only thing*
I sing along to

NO

I can feel the roughness
of your jeans
Your zipper on my shoulder
This lasts an hour

YES

I can feel you sleeping
Your chest goes slow
Minutes last long here
Saving time

RED HERRING

Your flesh calls my bluff
it says *easy tiger*
when I'm already easy
I could leave you
for defending a rapist
but I won't
because my socks boast RODEO QUEEN
and you could get any girl you want
right?

UNTITLED

Here eat this
The *c* is silent

LETTERS WITH MRS CHUNG

You're cute. Large round face. Questioning eyes.
Shiny new hair. I felt full at first. Your hands were soft,
but they felt like mine too. And then, over the years,
those questioning eyes became closed off, you didn't
look at me anymore. I wondered what I had done
wrong, I missed you. You didn't like the things I bought
you anymore, the things I cooked. You used to love
riding in the car with me. Then something happened,
and I wasn't company anymore, I was a way to get
somewhere. You only looked out the window. You
were mad that I didn't like to turn on the radio. I asked
you what you were doing later, tonight or in two years.
Everything was a one word answer and I began to
think I didn't like you very much. And then, just as I
was wishing you'd leave, you did. I wanted you to
come back, even if just to sit in the car, with the radio
or without. I felt heavy because you weren't doing
anything. I called you at night sometimes and you
were out. *I'm sorry,* I'd say, and sometimes I'd cry. I'm
sorry that maybe it didn't turn out right, maybe I wasn't
good enough, and now what will you do. You'd be out
with your boyfriend and the crying made you
uncomfortable. You'd tell me *it's okay, I had a nice
time when I was young* and then you'd hang up on me
when I asked, What will you do?

You're the most beautiful woman in the world. I'm young but I can tell that you are because people treat you differently. My tiny body then felt even bigger than it does now, I think because I felt safe. When I was tired, you'd pick me up and your hands were warm. And then, after some years, there was somebody else for you to pick up, and besides, I was getting too heavy. Sometimes though, you'd hold my hand when we were in big crowds or at the mall. I was afraid that other kids would see and that worried me, they were already wearing bras with tiny rosebuds. I wriggled out and hoped your feelings weren't hurt. When I turned the radio on, you turned it off. I sang *"Give me just one night, una noche"* and you snapped *You don't even know what that means.* You bought me the first Britney CD. I remember screaming at you one Thanksgiving. You asked me what I was doing later, tonight or in two years. I didn't want what you wanted. I packed some books and underwear and left in the car you bought me. I felt very heavy, I thought maybe there was someone else you could pick up. You called me at night sometimes and I was out. You were crying and saying sorry, do you think it's too late for me? I would try to tell you *You were so good* but it made my voice go funny and it was hard to talk over your crying. You asked me if I had enough money and I lied, Of course I do.

POV

She's got hair like a wide tooth comb
big smiles all winter
she tells me
when I'm rich I'll never drive drunk
you neither
we'll use all the olive oil we want
wipe our butts with fresh loaves
sourdough and rosemary
Until then
I'll be thinking about need and want
You and your utensils

INTIMACY

You lay the towel smooth
it out
a lovers' picnic
tendering bloodbath warming
Your sheets are covered in these
deals
But this one is new
Another thing
I have too much of

MEAN ASHTRAY

You are a girl that's really good
at losing things
in the yellow morning
flush with knowing
we won't be moving much
there are gaps in your bangs and
black crumbs on your cheek
that I would eat up if we were not so full
on eight dollar chocolates
counting quarters
black cats licking each other
shaking your hat at gas stations
emphatic
hissing *it's all fiction*
You groan
reminding me of warm water
You can't take me home so
your long arms hold me twice

RENT CONTROL

You never liked simulating pussy
but you let that animal
sit on your shoulder all day long
You won a t-shirt for screaming the loudest
but they didn't let you into their college
We told Putin *cut it out*
We love the house but we can't give you
all our money

RED

do you like me because
I am soft
and ask what color Gatorade
or do you like me because
I am here
and can be hurt

MOUTH FULL

at JonBenet's house her teeth
are tiny gravestones
you sing to me
downtown
where all the lights are bright
the car stalls and the monkey man
on autopilot
gives me a high-five

TAB

She climbs on top of me
closes the door, puts her shit
in my mouth
even to me this feels
lackluster
What do you want me to do
with four bags of fat?
She has a cold and a little hot tongue
flicking
but I'm wondering about the man in her kitchen
I take back my tongue she shrugs
There will always be another hot rod

CORNBREAD AND WAR NEVER CHANGE

The first world war and your own
seem the same
He stuck a glass banana up his ass
It was a display banana
Is it easy to be man
Is it easy to be banana

2000s

We go without underwear
unless our mothers buy some
for the holidays
and take the tequila out of our hands

EATING

My prettiest friend replaces
my molding shower curtain in exchange
for one skinny marg
You eat my four day old pussy
and I wonder
if it's out of politeness
a most mild fuck
An old-fashioned gal is here to please
Do you miss the
devolution
what we're used to
well do you
do you
I'm trying to get in good
with the waitress
but when she comes
my mouth is full

UNTITLED

Fender bender
Everything's okay
The fat cop says OKEY DOKEY
You are the tin man

WANTED

A young hottie to clean, iron
A form-fitting backpack
Is this what you want
Is this why
you're always trying to take back
that rib
You think it's yours
We're made for you?
A scowl and a grade older
someone pulls me away from the tv
my bad eyes pressed up against it
watching USA's version of Helen of Troy
Diane Kruger looks sad in her first big movie
The bathroom sink is the right height
for me to press up against it
and want something to be taken from me
I want
the petal pink shoes
I want what my name means
but this is how we grow
whipping out our clits in kindergarten class
saying I HAVE A PENIS TOO

YOU MARRIED YOUR FIRST BOYFRIEND

You bought a house
with a marble shower for your dog
that will eventually chew
on your newborn's
soft spot

DO YOU BELIEVE IN GOD

tiny waves crisp offshore
peaking
squatting, you have olive rings on every finger

at the last minute
you decided not to come

THE YOLK DOESN'T TASTE THE SAME IF YOU DON'T CLOSE YOUR EYES

We wrap our babies in newspaper
and lick them clean
The fat is good for us
We wait for our owners to do something
bad
so that we can be unhappy
Leave the boy to his egg
soft
It will only be a minute

POTENTIAL

When's the last time
you drew a dick
I mean
a really good one
When's the last time
you felt like this

JONAS

Full hams strung up
in the window
He's vegan, haunting
that cop he hates
I'm dreaming of a salmon bagel
moving faster than the clouds now
Your fingers in my mouth
machine in the sky
cuts through like water
Is it easier?

UNTITLED

Something's wrong with my dog
shrieking
a skinned hand
extends a crooked finger
a pearly pink cone
You're only six
but you laugh with dad

THANK YOU GUCCI

You only listen to songs about
bustin nuts
but who am I
too high and always inadequate
How can I tell you
I can never love you

You turn the wine upside down
to see if it's empty
I play dead and stutter mister
Of course they like you more
I wish I could wake up first so I
could leave
Quiet

ANIMALS

You pin me to the wall
I didn't ask for this
You tell me you're going to cum
all over my face
I hurry
to write my name
on all the water bottles
before anyone gets comfortable

JUNGLE MAN

The ground is hard packed
dirt, pushing back as we run
We must catch the fruit or else
it will be tomorrow
The truck's splitting siren
Managua Managua Managua!
a comfort
Manzana, naranja! and others
I forget
You feed me
sticky tamarind from the trees
where we sleep
where we were robbed
The hole in the fence is still there
I lick the pulp from your fingers
A man
Now you squeeze choice fruit
before we wrap the winners in my shirt
a handsome apple
Alto alto! the fruit man
frantic
All the fruit is good until you squeeze it
We turn and
the ground pushes back

DANCING SITTING

Want to see some ugly
pies I made?
Want to see a floating head
a black eye
You say OH I LOVE FAULKNER
you dumb boy
You're just as beautiful
even wrapped in latex

PRAYER

Making deals with god
in the bathroom
always your bathroom, your eyes
ballooning
you turn down the song and say
I want everything to be okay
but you're eating a peanut butter sandwich
clueless
The rat on the other side of the wall
is getting bigger
and more powerful

BLUES

Her name is Blue
and everything about her is long
She snakes round your back
and says Isn't it two-for-one here
The bartender agrees
I've got my millionth drink
and my millionth chip

JEFF WILL SMOKE YOUR WEED BUT HE WON'T LIKE IT

My baby his name
is Long Egg
anyway you cut it
we're listening to metal and
eating a cheese plate I made
with no cheese
You work around the carrots

OVEREASY

Working reeking
sucking
We're splitting tabs and killing babies
because
what's love
You say I have a bit of a belly
but you swear it's cute
Your devolution is fed by your salty
cum
but I still think of you in the hot morning
when I make eggs for my new boyfriend

LYLE AND DIVISION

The street light flicks
off
like my phone
I wake in my head shaking
full of cat treats
a gold silver bullet
with my tax return hand
exploding

JANUARY

I bite my nails and bring home bread
I finally have beer money
Have you forgotten about me
yet
I hope it's ok
I hope you're ok

UNTITLED

Please don't take me to jail
I have popsicles in the car
and this light takes too long

NO 1 CHINESE

Everytime I come over
you draw Kobe
but you can't get the head right
I want to leave
again
but someone's in the kitchen
Did she really say no?
Did she mean it?
with intention
It's just a matter of which
of your roommates are worse

LITE

We are cold sores
sleeping with meek men
out of meekness
he drove all this way
something about a shilling in a cup
and that's war
when the beer's gone

HUMAN

Your boner for missing kids
makes me wonder
what it is about me
that gets you off
The neighbors get on
the nightly news and
try not to smile
but the dog gives it away

SOUNDS WE MAKE

Damn it all sounds
hollow
as fuck
Me knocking watermelons
someone tells me it should sound
like wood
You knocking on your wood paneled walls
We don't know what we're looking for

FOR THE LAST WEEK I'VE BEEN A GOOD PERSON

Your womb is so cold
Your room is so cold
I'll meet you in the bathroom

EVERY SONG SOUNDS LIKE THE ONE FROM PEANUTS

I sell my purity ring for the last piece of fruit
Your friend at the counter says
Put it on my tab
but what does that mean
It means I'm stupid
I will dump anyone

HAPPY SIX MONTHS

That Jesus Only tabernacle
you know the one
near the end of Dortch Street
you ran over that squirrel one afternoon
you let it ruin the mood

TEQUILA TIME

The only problem is his stare
and then everything
else
Every hour on the hour
he asks me *que hora es*
is it worth it
does it matter
The skinny boy pokes me
with a pool stick he says
You're either a witch or dead the way you're sleeping
I smile at him I hate myself for it
He shrugs out of his skin and wins the game

JUDITH B

He's weak the narrator says
He's weak you repeat
you whisper to me
I adore him for his simplicity his flatness
sketched
They drank my wine I wheedle
no angles shadows depth
He's asking for a literal translation
by the time I'm out of the bathroom
He's pulled up Rotten Tomatoes
Of course he's a Pisces
No one
will love me
more
I try to tell him about reader-response
but he's masturbating to memories

A BIG TWIN BED

Do you remember when I called you kid
It was warmer outside then
We locked the doors and I swore
I'd never
share a vacation with anyone again
You snoring
pissy
My toes are cold
and what you give me
isn't enough
Remember when your high cheekbones
got you love
kid

BOY

Saving up all your life to hit someone
You think kink
is tickling my feet in the middle
You take your work boots off
and wait
for me to get hot

JAIL COOKIE

What did that dream mean in which I refused
to save anyone but myself?
skin stretched thin and translucent
She's got nice wide hips and I hope he's happy
what is a second to her, to him
The last day I didn't worry about my mother
or father or the making of me
I wonder about the free catheters on tv
headphones that crackle
reading the word of god but really
just masturbating to Song of Solomon
the JC Penney catalog
yet to sprout my own tits but something
about those flaps on maternity bras
they give me pains
How will I hug my family once I'm a woman?
I get my period
finally
the arresting officer tips his hat
and says gracious
Welcome to the Gray Bar Motel

YOU PICKED THE WRONG BED

The car's stopped in a field
the sun blistering the silver exterior
a slippery frog takes everyone's eye
the Aussie has disappeared and Now
frog is wearing a crown of flowers
Liz coos *how cute* and dumps my leftovers in the grass
no holes in the tupperware
we drive away frog looks sick, maybe
the flowers are too heavy
if there are holes where will we keep our lunch
frog is dead Liz says dumping the leftovers
in my mouth
I lean out the window a slippery frog falls out
we've got to go back for the Aussie someone cries
from the backseat
I know where she is

WINNERS AND LOSERS

Shameless gallows hung
with hockey flags
We lose but no one moves
to take their Christmas lights down
Ball players
spit
slap each ass cheek
and say FAG

PRODUCER

Imagine that hot brown apple
steaming winter
Rick wants to save somebody
but not that much

WASH N DRY

I ask you for laundry money
lying in your lap
praying for a flat tummy
How can you love me like this?

We laugh at Late Nite
like we mean it
Missiles are headed for Guam but
they keep fishing
We all look the same in that second

RICH

my baby's got powder sugar hair
churro bod
she loves eating at gas stations
especially the sit down kind

I WILL HATE YOU ONCE MY PERIOD BLOOD WASHES OUT

Look at me
You're looking through my phone
as I sleep
You ask me
when I took that picture
ashing in that seashell
You don't realize that nothing
is for sex
but thanks for reminding me
that my dad's house is haunted
the laptop keeps scrolling
doors flying open
shrieking
try our new double chalupa

LÓPEZ CATALÁN

blossoms taunting, velvet veins
and chalk flowers
This wood grain contains
the history of the universe
and your sun-warmed brick
feels like flesh

FAST

In *BUTTERMILK TENDERS* the *E*'s
are just *3*'s backward
You tell me this and lick
your lips
but not him
He thinks every girl is the girl
from Parks and Rec
The cat purring
You don't care what I tell the kids

THE ETERNAL APPLE

He talks about the status of his hunger
it's irrelevant
subject to the mood
I feel far
away
Bump your glasses up your nose
something white streaks the sky and my dog
drinks black water
Look at the way those children look at each other
before we all become ugly in our sleep
before all the kitchens get smaller
with us sitting tight at the table

NO ONE IS OK

I check my braces and I'm still ugly
Someone tells me they beheaded that American
soldier today
Dad nods and says
It took a whole thirty seconds for him to stop screaming
He peels the wrapper from his muffin

HIGH THREAD COUNT

He comes and says *you hate me*
don't you
I don't answer, his face is too close to mine
He leaves the room to find something to clean up with
I ask *did you pull out in time*
and I try to recall what he looks like
There it is, sharp eyes, baby blue, pinched mouth
Everything is projection he says he says
but I haven't opened my mouth yet
I take another drink and one, wonder
what I look like from your side
that's so cute that you ask every time
but that doesn't answer my question

PALM TREES

To get a reaction
he pulls his dick faster Now
gets up to get a paper towel
Are you ready kids?
eating outside has made us
harder to relate to
the couple next door we can hear
the soft sheets
the alarm goes off
I've never hated anyone more
even in paradise
You are mild even in
disappointing me

SOMEONE ELSE CAME UP WITH IT FIRST

It's ok to get fucked hard on the carpet
sometimes
lips parted
It's not a big deal that your bones break
a bald spot in the sunroof
do you remember
the way George yelled at mom
at that blinking red light
that four way stop
tentative
He is the worse kind of us

CAT

Is that a huge sagebrush
Is everyone hitting on me
Maybe that's the joke
my hoe
I say it unnatural
I say it to your ex-girlfriend
but I figure it's kosher
because she's blonde now

DRINKS WITH AN EX

Fat Joe isn't fat anymore
but still softly talking pussy
I want to know
does that chickpea get you as hard
as I used to?
You want to unfollow the bartender
because he's full of himself but then
where
will you
drink
I mean, we will smoke anything if we have nothing
You and me
sitting in olive brine
waiting on the big pimento

FUCK MORE

Hands on a creamy coral cup
Its own personality
Your fingers trace my back and
I'd rather not respond, I'd rather
not drink
but I put on a dress for this
a dog for distraction
pick a helmet seems a weary line
and we both know it
after it's here
We carry soft spine books
that you eventually collect
out of impatience
You like the sketch I did of you
because it's easy
one long line fumbling
fucking more
you finish my sentence and
it's more vulgar than what I had coming
I get drunk and go home
out the side door

A WELCOME MELON

Stir up my insides
Fill your fritters with
the last of summer
Do you poop in front of him?
The sun sinks and I digest
the last bad date

A GOOD SIGN

my first body spray was juniper breeze
the summer the gun store burned down
for the second time
a sunroof was what we were saving for
bending over
in front of the mirror

YOU BOUGHT ME SUNGLASSES IN THE CITY

Hire me baby
I got grown out bangs
pinned back
that I hate
I'm peeing in a mug to throw
out my fourth floor window

Hands up
with people looking
do you feel like Cher yet?

THE PILOT IS MAKING SMALL TALK BESIDE ME

His mouth hanging open
tells me to wake up
These squealing midnight pigs
hanging and red
A red tie on his white shirt
The others know
and the meat is tough

NOW

Everything but the bagel
a workshop for our grieving hangover
Can we have unrequited love
the only kind
in a time of wi-fi

UNTITLED

small brown wings
dancing down
how bad can you be with money

ADRIENNE

two for you, one for me
what time is it
my eyes bulge
it's morning, a dog yawns
a leaf falls in the drying shed

MIDTOWN

These soft lesbians
careening
flippant
offering weak words of
early morning
No, you didn't wake us up last night

ARE YOU LISTENING

Two of my pillows don't even
equal one of yours
You tell me to take my contacts out
in my sleep
I try to bite your hand
the one with the cash
That POV porn
he put it in her ass
but we cried because we could hear the rain
on the windows
He's cumming now
all over his argyle sweater
I have plenty of things to do
other than this

IS IT IN YET

We're always worried about
the big cake
yours is pink and pretty
matching forks
a girl you went to high school with
draws a heart
and you still melt
Good for nothing